NO HANDS, NO EXCUSES:

Living A No Excuses Life
No Matter What Happens To You

NO HANDS, NO EXCUSES:

Living A No Excuses Life
No Matter What Happens To You

BY LEE SHELBY

Dedication

I WOULD BE remiss if I did not give glory to God for allowing me to survive a tragic accident on August 12, 1991, that could have taken my life. Because God had a higher purpose for me, I am still here.

I especially want to dedicate this book to my beautiful, wonderful wife Sherrie who has been a part of my life for twenty years. You are my better half and I am a better man because of you. You have loved me unconditionally from the beginning through everything, and without your support, I would not be where I am today.

I also dedicate this book to my three wonderful children LeAnna, Lauren, and Zach, along with Eli, Abby, Deian, and John Henry, four of the most awesome grandchildren in the world.

I further want to dedicate this book to the two best parents a man could ever ask for, Joyce and Gilbert Shelby. From the beginning of my life, you helped shape and mold me to be the man I am today. You taught me respect, courage, the importance of family, and to have a great work ethic. You've been there with me through the good times and the bad, never giving up on me, and always helping me to create the attitude of never giving up or quitting.

Finally, this book is dedicated to one of the greatest men I've ever known and best friend I ever had, my grandfather Howard Jones. You taught me to love the Lord, along with so many life lessons. I miss you, and my love for you is still strong even though you have left this earth.

With Love and Blessings,

Lee Shelby

What People Are Saying About Lee Shelby...

OVER THE PAST five years, I have had the pleasure of getting to know Lee, both professionally and personally. I consider Lee a good friend and an awesome human being. Lee's passion for life and ever-present positive attitude is infectious. His ability to overcome and thrive after experiencing a life-altering workplace injury is a powerful testament of Lee's positive attitude and tenacity. These characteristics come out in all of Lee's interactions, whether as a motivational and safety speaker or in his one-on-one conversations with others.

A hallmark of a good friend is their authenticity and their ability to bring out the best in others. With Lee, what you see is what you get. He is a truly authentic person and a man of integrity. In all my interactions with Lee, he has consistently demonstrated his genuine care for other people by how he interacts with and encourages them to be the best versions of themselves. Lee encourages everyone he meets to look beyond whatever may be in front of them to see what can be, along with what needs to be done today to create the future they want.

I encourage everyone reading this to continue on into this book. Get to know Lee as I have. Hopefully, the message within will have a positive impact on your life as Lee's friendship has had on mine.

Ricardo "Rick" Aguilar, PHR, SHRM-CP, CUSP
Director of Talent Management & Development
Northeast Live Line Manager
Northline Utilities, LLC
Northeast Live Line, LLC

LEE IS ONE of the most inspirational men I have ever met. Lee suffered a horrific workplace accident that cost him both hands. Lee very easily could have lived on disability pay for the rest of his life but "average" is not in Lee's dictionary. Lee literally rebuilt his life from the ashes. Lee lives a "No Excuses" life 24-7 and is a man that NEVER backs down to any challenge. NEVER.

TC Bradley
CEO and Founder at Instant Celebrity Status

LEE IS A very special person, a gift from God, with a very simple message about life, choices, and consequences.

Denis Treacy
Chief Safety & Quality Officer, Pladis Global

LEE REPRESENTS EXCELLENCE. He uses his perspectives about an unfortunate disability to inspire others. His efforts save lives and limbs around the USA every day.

Bob Harris, CAE
Harris Management Group, Inc.

LEE LOST HIS hands in an industrial accident. However, he has accomplished more since his accident than most people will accomplish in a lifetime. If you want to motivate your staff to use all of its potential, then you need to hire Lee to speak to your entire workforce.

Jimmy Grubbs
Independent Investment Management Professional
No excuses. Keep moving forward. Simple and powerful.
Wanda Zayachkowski
Self-employed Entrepreneur

I HAVE WORKED with over a thousand organizations and have heard hundreds of speakers. Lee is the best motivational speaker I have seen.

Rick Vulpitta
NIPSCO Generation Safety

LEE'S STORY AND message are a game changer. His no excuses attitude is contagious. I can't imagine anyone not being inspired to live a no excuses life after hearing him speak.

Carolyn Olson
Certified Health Coach
Carolyn Olson Enterprises, LLC

LEE WAS ABLE to relate very well with the audience, was extremely effective, and added a very important personal touch. The feedback from those in attendance was absolutely outstanding and I will definitely hire Lee again! He is the consummate professional and is a genuine, honest person.

Michael Smith
Manager, Safety & Health at NV Energy

HIS MESSAGE IS one that will change you and invoke a greater resolve to make better choices.

Ted Allan
Met-Ed Director, Regional Ops Support

CONTENTS

Foreword

Lee Shelby's story had an immediate impact on me. He is the perfect example of triumph over tragedy, and I am proud to call him my friend. In 2016, I had the pleasure of meeting Lee at a corporate event for several hundred attendees at a public utility where we were both speakers. After hearing Lee's story, I was moved and inspired. I felt sad for what he had gone through and for the reality of what a challenge it must be on a daily basis to live without hands, but what he had accomplished since was inspiring. That same day, Lee also listened to my message, *The Gameplan for Aging, Your Four Quarters of Life*, a message designed to educate, motivate, and inspire people to strive towards living life with a positive attitude and a healthy body, mind, and spirit. My message is that poor lifestyle, genetic issues, and poor choices in life can be overcome. Unfortunately, many people *don't* feel that this kind of change is important enough to strive for, or they feel that they just *can't* make positive changes to their lives, which can result in too many people not even making it to retirement, or ending up with big health issues soon after retirement.

That day back in 2016, Lee and I were both inspired by the messages we heard, and over the next few years, Lee and I became good friends. We bonded over our similar views on living with a positive attitude through all life's twists and turns, and on faith, family, and a mutual respect for each other. We really enjoyed being in each other's company – even if it was through a phone call!

A few years ago, Lee told me that when he was traveling through airports, he would become winded and feel sluggish. Lee recognized that he needed to make a change (a new "*Gameplan to live*"), and he began taking better care of himself by eating right and becoming fit. At first, he said, he found himself making excuses due to his physical limitations, but once he made the commitment to dump those excuses, he went to the gym regularly and cleaned up his diet. Fit Lee can now accomplish even more and feel healthy and strong while doing it!

I know that there are many inspirational stories out there and folks similar to Lee; however, *No Hands, No Excuses* will leave a lasting impression on every reader with the motivation to stop making excuses and take immediate action to live life at its best. Life here as we know it is a temporary journey, and as long as you live life making excuses, it's virtually impossible to live the life you deserve.

Mark A. Everest
President, Occupational Athletics, Inc.
Author of *The Gameplan for Aging, Your Four Quarters of Life,*
Road Athlete, Occupational Athlete, Bus Athlete, Hunter Athlete
Sirius Radio XM on-air personality, Road Athlete, Channel 147

Introduction

The reason you have what you have is because that is what you have decided to settle for right now. Change your mind... change your life.

— *John Assaraf*

THIS BOOK IS designed to inspire you to live a *no excuses* life. I am going to challenge you to change your limiting beliefs, the stories you tell yourself, and most importantly, the excuses that stand in the way of you living your dreams.

I had the perfect excuse not to write a book. I have no hands. I'm a bilateral below the elbow amputee. I didn't let that stop me. This is my second book, and I'm already planning my third one. After my accident, I had the perfect excuse not to go back to work. I could have gone on disability. I didn't. Ten months after having both of my hands amputated, I went back to my job.

At twenty-eight years old, I made a mistake that changed my life forever. I could have played the victim. I could have let anger consume me. Instead, I committed to overcome my challenges and live my best life possible.

You have choices every single day when you wake up. Am I going to be a victim or a victor of my circumstances? Am I going to procrastinate, or am I going to take action? Am I going to doubt my abilities, or am I going to believe in myself? Am I going to step out of my comfort zone, or am I going to play it safe? You get to make the decision.

In the pages of this book, I will share my personal story of triumph over tragedy. I will challenge you to look at seven of the most common excuses people make that stand in the way of reaching their goals and dreams. You will learn to recognize and confront yourself so that you can break the cycle of excuses.

Everyone makes excuses. We are human. My intention is not for you to be perfect. It's for you to increase your awareness of why you make excuses. The more you understand when and why you make excuses, the better your chances will be to change your thought processes and behavior. My goal is for you to live your very best life without regret.

After reading this book, my hope is that you will challenge your beliefs about what you can achieve and what you are capable of accomplishing. Real change takes consistent effort and commitment. It takes alignment between your beliefs and goals. It's time to raise your standards and make an internal shift.

CHAPTER ONE
I Can't Because...

"Bad things do happen; how I respond to them defines my character and the quality of my life. I can choose to sit in perpetual sadness, immobilized by the gravity of my loss, or I can choose to rise from the pain and treasure the most precious gift I have... life itself."

— *Walter Anderson*

The Accident

On August 12, 1991, I made a decision that changed my life forever. At twenty-eight years old, I was an overhead lineman for a municipal utility company in Memphis, Tennessee. I had grown up watching my best friend's dad do line work, and it inspired me. I loved this job because it was exciting, it kept me outside, and the money was excellent. It was a dream job to me. There was nothing better than to stand on two inches of steel fifty feet off the ground or to hold thirteen thousand volts of electricity in my hands.

Part of my job was to install, repair, and remove overhead distribution power lines. On this particular morning, I was working to change out the service to a house up in a bucket truck. To handle high voltage electricity in your hands, you were supposed to wear the proper PPE (Personal Protective Equipment), so you could hold energized conductors in your hands. We called it rubber gloving. Instead of wearing my PPE, I had put on a pair of ordinary leather gloves. I was holding a pair of bolt cutters in a vertical position with my right hand over the left, and I accidentally touched the back of my right hand to a thirteen thousand, two hundred volt energized overhead conductor. Electricity entered my right hand, traveled through the right handle of the bolt cutters into the left handle and into my left hand. Under my left armpit, there was an exit wound from the electricity traveling through my body. The bolt cutters blew up in my hands, and I collapsed into the bucket.

When the line had blown, it sounded like a stick of dynamite exploding. My ears were ringing so loud that the only thing I could hear was my heartbeat. It created an arc flash that affected my vision. There were five guys from my crew on the ground hollering to me, but I couldn't hear a thing. Since I had collapsed to the floor of the bucket, my knees were at my chest pressed against the wall. My arms were over my head. My crew couldn't see me or communicate with me.

I had a conversation with one of the guys on my crew named Brian later after the incident. He was working seventy feet away from me. He had been standing at the top of a new pole we had just set. He saw me touch the thirteen thousand volt conductor. He said when I dropped, he felt like he knew I was already dead. He wasn't sure what he would find when he got to me.

At that point, two men jumped on the bucket truck to maneuver the bucket I was in down to the ground with the assumption I wasn't alive. When I reached the bottom, to their surprise, I was coherent enough to respond when they asked if I was okay. I told them I couldn't stand because I was physically wedged down into the bucket. They helped me get out, and then I was able to walk to sit down in the grass. I was in shock at this point and not feeling much pain.

I sat there with my burned hands in my lap trying to get them to move to take my gloves off, but they wouldn't operate. This was the moment when I started to worry. I picked up my left hand, and it just fell over my wrist. I sat there and let my eyes adjust. I noticed that there was smoke coming out of the cuff of my left glove. I was worried before, but now I was really worried. One of the guys on my crew had to pull off my gloves because my hands were still burning. There was no time to wait for the paramedics. He had to pull off both gloves immediately before the burns worsened.

When the first responders arrived at the scene, they saw that my buddy Brian was taking care of me. Luckily, he had some EMT training. They immediately assisted him by applying burn sheets and rinsing my wounds with sterile water until the ambulance arrived from Memphis.

Thirteen thousand, two hundred volts had passed through my unprotected hands. My hands looked like they had been put in a microwave, dehydrated, and then cauterized from the wrist down. They were curled up in a clenched fist like when they were holding the bolt cutters.

The volunteer fire department in that little town answered my emergency call. What that meant for me was the volunteer jumped in his pick-up truck and drove over to the site. It took the ambulance twelve to thirteen minutes to get to the scene.

Immediately they decided to transport me by helicopter to the hospital to the medical burn unit in Memphis. Halfway through the helicopter ride, the feeling in my hands started to come back. It felt like I was holding onto the coils of a hot stove. It was excruciating.

When I reached the hospital, I met with a trauma plastic surgeon and an occupational therapist. I knew they were going to have to amputate my hands, but I asked them to do everything they could to save them. The doctor promised me he would not amputate them on this day, but he couldn't guarantee that it wouldn't happen. The main concern was keeping me alive.

I had six surgeries over the next five days. After each surgery, I was brought back to my room and laid flat on my back. There was a suspension frame around my bed so that my arms could be suspended with a special netting above my head to keep the swelling down. Unfortunately, the medical team was unable to save my hands. They had to be amputated mid-forearm. I spent twenty-three days in the intensive burn unit recovering.

After I was released, I spent seven months in occupational therapy and rehabilitation. I had to relearn everything. Instead of hands, I now had prosthetic hooks. My accident was a tragedy, but I had a choice. I could make excuses and sink into depression, or I could forge ahead and learn how to live my life without hands. I was twenty-eight years old, and now I had to learn how to do everything from eating, bathing, and using the restroom with hooks instead of hands.

Was this out of my comfort zone? You bet it was, but I wasn't willing to let the challenges get me down. I didn't want anyone else to have to take care of me. I wanted to get back to living my life. My occupational therapist helped me to do that.

The Excuse Zone

Let's talk about your comfort zone. Your comfort zone is where you feel safe. It gives you a sense of control. The problem with staying in your comfort zone is that you aren't growing. If you have goals you want to achieve, you must be willing to go through some challenges. You have to improve and learn a new set of skills. If you are not willing to get a little uncomfortable, there's not much room for growth.

Here's what happens to most people. They dip their toe in the water. It feels cold, so they stay where it's warm. What they don't realize is if they jumped in, they would get used to it. It would become their new comfort zone.

Getting out of your comfort zone starts with a decision. Then, it's your commitment to stay the course no matter how uncomfortable it feels. When you lack the inner knowing that you can accomplish your goal or dream, you live in doubt. You doubt your ability to tackle whatever comes your way. Doubt breeds fear.

Fear is what leads to the excuse zone. You will make up excuses not to take action because the outcome is unknown. You don't know what will happen if you leave the job you hate, so you use that as an excuse to stay comfortably uncomfortable.

Here are some of the effects of living in fear:

- lack of self-confidence
- let other people's opinions affect you
- settle for less than you deserve or desire
- compromise your dreams
- don't speak up
- procrastination
- turn to food, drugs, alcohol, television, or other addictions

When fear dominates your life, you live in stress and worry. Whatever you focus on expands.

Ask yourself right now:

Where is my focus?

do I hold in my mind?

What repetitive thoughts and emotions do I experience?

Fear is an emotion. It's a survival mechanism. When it comes to going after your goals, there is no lion waiting to pounce. You have to be willing to experience the fear, but still take action.

Many people get stuck because they fear failure. They don't want to be a disappointment or to look bad. What they don't understand is that they fail by not starting. The only way you fail is by not pushing forward. You may not make a goal by a chosen date, but why let that stop you from continuing the journey?

Taking a wrong turn or falling short of a goal is part of the learning process. To let go of excuses, you have to be willing to let yourself make mistakes. Your personal growth comes from the challenges you encounter. The challenges allow you to acquire new skills and expand your comfort zone. Give yourself a break. You don't have to be perfect. It's okay for things to get a little messy. Let go of perfection and be productive. When you let go of excuses, you allow room for growth.

The Truth About *I Can't Because...*

Did you know your brain listens to everything you say? If you say, "I can't," then your brain believes you. *I can't* tells your brain you have no control. If you want to live an excuse free life, erase *I can't* from your vocabulary. Don't underestimate the power of your words.

The truth of the matter is that when you say you can't do something, you are choosing not to do it. Is it that you can't do it, or is it that you won't do it?

"Oh, I can't start a business now. I have too many obligations."

Wrong. You won't start a business because you are not willing to prioritize your obligations.

"I can't work out in the morning. I don't have the time."

Wrong. You won't work out in the morning because you are not willing to change your routine.

"I can't go to the party."

Wrong. You can go, but you are choosing not to go because you have something else you place of higher importance.

"I can't go back to school. I'm too old for that."

Wrong. You can go back. I guarantee the school will accept your money no matter what your age.

Using *I can't* is an easy way to stay in the excuse zone. It comes down to this. If you think you can't, you're right. If you think you can, you're right too. Which is it going to be?

As you continue reading this book, I want you to consider how the words you speak aloud and the dialogue you create in your mind affect your reality. Your words are a powerful force. They can heal or hurt. They can help or hinder. Consider what you are training your mind to believe. Are your words currently helping you to live excuse free, or are they keeping you in the excuse zone?

Leaving the Excuse Zone

Recently, I wanted to tighten up my diet. I travel frequently speaking all over the United States and internationally as well. I found myself putting on a few extra pounds and struggling to get through airports. I decided to change my situation. I started working with a trainer at the gym. I set a workout routine that included weight training and cardio. As I progressed, I realized that what I was eating was affecting my progress. I started working with a health coach and was inspired to make changes to my eating habits.

After a few weeks, I wasn't following the plan. I wanted to

make the shift, but the plan wasn't quite working the way I had hoped. I went back to my coach and told her about the challenges I was having. She immediately called me out and said, "Lee, sounds like you have a lot of excuses." She was right. I bought into the new plan for eating healthy on the road, but I didn't get myself organized and prepared for a new routine.

We talked through some ways I could organize bringing my food with me. I had to create a system to stay on track. I was winging it, and it wasn't working. It would take some preparation before I traveled, but because I was committed to reaching my health goals, it was worth it.

We all make excuses when something is out of our routine or our comfort zone at one time or another. It happens to me. But, I have trained myself to catch myself when I am doing it. It's a matter of raising your consciousness so that you are aware of when you make an excuse. I'm not perfect, and I don't expect myself to be. But what I do expect is that every day I make an effort to let go of excuses and make progress toward my goals.

Ask Yourself

1. In what areas of my life am I using the excuse *I can't*?

2. How are my *I can't* excuses stopping me from reaching my goals?

3. What step can I take today to change my *I can't* mindset?

CHAPTER TWO
I'm Not Ready...

"Inaction breeds doubt and fear. Action breeds confidence and courage. If you want to conquer fear, do not sit home and think about it. Go out and get busy."

— *Dale Carnegie*

Back to Work

I'D BEEN OFF work for ten months and twenty-three days. I didn't want to sit home any longer. I didn't want someone to take care of me. I wanted to go back to work and feel normal again. I wasn't able to work in the capacity of a lineman. Metal hooks created too many challenges when working on power lines. My supervisor gave me a pickup truck and a radio. I started with simple duties. I ran errands for crews until they could figure out where to place me. Eventually, I took on the role of an inspector.

Going back to work was part of the relearning process. I had to learn to drive again, plus there was no GPS at that time. I would drive all over the city with my map book in my lap using the old-fashioned way of getting from here to there. I had to learn how to use my prosthetics to work the hand-held radio. It had little knobs to turn it on and off as well as to change the channels. Pressing the button to talk was challenging without fingers. There were physical tasks that required me to lift supplies and equipment, then load them into the truck and deliver them to crews. I also had to write with my prosthetics. Although these elementary tasks were challenging at first, I adapted. I was grateful to get back to work. It was an opportunity to be a functional part of society.

Once I became an inspector, part of my job duties were to inspect all of the steel transmission structures in our county. The steel towers and steel pole structures had to be inspected from the air. This meant I would go to the local police department to rent one of their helicopters. A pilot would be hired to take me to the areas for inspection. This type of aerial inspection wasn't cheap for the company. They were looking for alternatives to reduce costs and I was approached about taking flying lessons in a single engine fixed wing aircraft.

I agreed and then went to Olive Branch Airport in Olive Branch Mississippi. I learned to fly with no hands and no assistive apparatus. There were challenges, but the biggest one was operating the radio. It was hard to hold the airplane yolk and also hold and press the button on the receiver to talk. The planes were newer, so they had a GPS navigation system, but my instructor wanted me to learn the old school way. He taught me how to use a compass and a map. Getting my license was one of the most challenging parts of the process. You have to be fingerprinted, but I don't have fingerprints. Nevertheless, I got my license and became a pilot.

Returning to work wasn't so much about my physical capabilities. It was about my mindset. I went back to work with the ambition and determination to put my life back together. I was driven to break barriers. I believe people could feel that energy from me.

When I was in the hospital, a friend of mine that had worked with me at the utility company came to visit. He thought he was coming there to lift me up. He was feeling terrible about the accident and me losing both of my hands. Not knowing what to expect when he walked through the door of my hospital room, he found me smiling and in good spirits. He could tell I was glad to see him. We sat, talked, laughed, and carried on. Years later, he let me know that my positive attitude lifted him that day because of my good spirits.

It took my family, the people I worked with, and my friends a little time to get used to seeing me with no hands. They didn't know how to act at first. I believe that my demeanor and no excuses attitude helped to set everyone at ease and be more comfortable around me. I had an *I'm ready* mindset, and that's how I approached going back to work.

The Truth About *I'm Not Ready*

Many people aren't willing to start a new project or work on a new goal if they can't do it perfectly. They don't trust themselves to do a good job. The truth is this is a self-esteem issue. If you don't believe you are good enough, you will have a strong tendency to avoid what is uncomfortable. You will shelter your ego and focus on what is in your comfort zone. Procrastination can become chronic because you avoid the perceived pain of doing a task.

Self-doubt is a major cause of procrastination. You feel like you are not ready so you will read more books, take another class, or go to a seminar. People get stuck in the learning phase and don't put the new knowledge into practice. They are focused on doing something right or doing it perfectly instead of being effective. Negative consequences don't have to be your driving force to take action. You don't have to wait until you are desperate or a tragedy strikes to get started.

When you continually put things off until later, you create a buildup of stress. Stress then leads to feelings of anxiety, guilt, and shame. This emotional state can spiral into depression. It's a slippery slope when you let excuses become a way of life.

You have the power to change right now. Make a list of the tasks, goals, and dreams where procrastination caused you not to take action. When you write them on paper, it helps you to release all of the pressure built up from holding them in your mind. Now that they are on paper, you don't have the task of remembering everything that needs to be done. Could you choose one item each day that you have been putting off to complete? Could you choose a major goal and take one action daily toward reaching that goal? Once you let go of how difficult or how big that task seems, your mind can accept doing one small thing. Over time, each daily action compounds.

Shoulding on Yourself

When you tell yourself you are not ready to start a goal or task, it can often be accompanied by feeling guilty. People tend to *should* on themselves. *I'm not ready, but I should lose weight, get out of this relationship, clean the house, do my taxes, or whatever else you are avoiding.* When you don't take action, there is a tendency to feel bad about yourself. *Should* is a judgment about you not being good enough. When you feel not good enough, it will affect your self-esteem.

You cannot *should* yourself to force action to happen. It does the opposite. It reinforces your inactivity. Ask yourself where the *should* originates. Is it something you want to do but aren't, or is it something a family member or society says you should do?

Rather than *should, must,* or *ought to,* use *prefer to, want to,* or *choose to.* Whenever the words *should, must,* or *ought to* appear in our language, it's usually a sign that we're putting pressure on ourselves or holding ourselves to an arbitrary standard. Often, when we tell ourselves we should or must do something, we wind up feeling unpleasant emotions like guilt, anxiety, or even shame. But we can achieve the same ends, with far less collateral emotional damage, by simply using more self-empowering language.[1]

In chapter one, I talked about how your word choice affects your brain. Removing the word *should* from your vocabulary will help you to change your thought patterns. Excuses are not physical. They are mental. Changing your language and how you speak to yourself is part of the process to release excuse-making behavior.

I never told myself, "I should go back to work." I wanted to get back to living life. I didn't *should* myself into it. There was no putting it off until tomorrow. For many people, tomorrow never comes. It's a lie you tell yourself to avoid the responsibility for your goals and dreams. When is now the right time to start?

Ask Yourself

1. In what areas of my life am I using the excuse *I'm not ready*?

2. What triggers me to feel I am not ready?

3. What's the story I tell myself when I feel I am not ready to start on a goal?

CHAPTER THREE
I Don't Know How...

"There's a difference between interest and commitment. When you're interested in doing something, you do it only when it's convenient. When you're committed to something, you accept no excuses; only results."

— *Kenneth Blanchard*

Diaper Duty

MY FIRST CHILD, LeAnna, was born fourteen months after my accident. When my occupational therapist found out my wife was pregnant, she called to tell me I had to come back to therapy. She wanted to teach me how to change diapers. I told her as I raised both prosthetics in the air, "This is the only positive thing that has come out of this so far… that I will never have to change a diaper." I thought I was off the hook for diaper duty. Yes, the pun is intentional.

My occupational therapist wouldn't accept my excuses. I gave in, and back to therapy I went. Changing diapers isn't anyone's favorite chore, but that was no excuse for hiding behind having no hands. My therapist presented me with a doll. She put it on the table along with a stack of diapers. The diapers had sticky tape, which was a challenge because they kept sticking to my hooks, the doll, and the table. This task was no easy feat for me. I finally got the process down when my therapist decided to kick the challenge up a notch. She brought over a real live child for practice. Needless to say, I was a diaper-changing dad. No excuses.

The Truth About *I Don't Know How*

There were a lot of things I didn't know how to do after my accident changed my life. Buttoning a pair of blue jeans was a concern. Sure, I could have said I don't know how so I'll just wear elastic band pants. No way! I'm a regular guy, and I wanted to wear jeans. I discussed this with my occupational therapist, and we created a tool for me to get them fastened. I didn't let not knowing how to do something stop me. I had the will, and I found a way.

Fishing had been one of my long-time hobbies. My occupational therapist worked with me so I could learn how to fish again. That meant I had to do it all. I learned to bait the hook, cast, reel it in, and take the fish off the hook. I didn't know how I was going to do it, but that is not the point. The point is that I was going to figure it out and she helped me to do it.

When you start to learn anything new, it can feel uncomfortable. It can be frustrating. You tend to put expectations on yourself that you have to be good at it right now. That's not how it works. Think about baseball. On day one, does the coach have you swing the bat at a ninety-five mile an hour fastball? Heck no! You have to start with the basics. You have to build a new skill set, practice them, and build upon them until they are mastered.

What about learning to play the piano? You are going to start with *Mary Had a Little Lamb* before you can play Mozart. The same goes for a new career. If you want to be a teacher, it takes at least four years of school plus doing your student teaching. You still won't be an expert. You'll learn more while on the job than you will when you train for it. There are situations you will face where you will have to learn on the fly. You will have to adapt and adjust. If you are a teacher, you don't encounter a challenging situation and say, "Bye, kids. I don't know how to handle this, so I'm going home for the day."

I don't know how is an excuse. It's an excuse not to push your limits. What you are really saying is, *I'm not willing to learn. I'm not willing to make mistakes. I'm not willing to be bad at something for a while. I'm not willing to deal with the uncomfortable emotions that come with trying something new.*

My physical therapist gave me a pad of paper, a pen, and an encyclopedia. She told me to start copying the book. No hands mean I can't write. Well, not exactly. I didn't know how, but it was time to learn to write by holding the pen in my prosthetic hook. Copying an encyclopedia wasn't fun, but I was committed to learning to write.

There were times in therapy that groups of the patients would go on field trips. One time, we went to the Mid-South Fair in Memphis. My therapist gave me the job of pushing someone who was in a wheelchair, because the person couldn't maneuver around without assistance. It was challenging considering I was only a few months into my occupational therapy. I had to take care of this person even though I seemed like an unlikely candidate. It was an important job, and I figured it out so the person could enjoy the outing. I knew people would be watching me, but I was willing to rise to the challenge and push past my comfort zone.

Sometimes it takes some adaptations to be able to do something you don't know how to do or think you can't do. I can drive a car because I got an assistive driving knob that is attached to the steering wheel. I can go where I want to go because I was willing to adapt and adjust to my situation. That's how life is. You have to adapt and adjust when you don't know how to do something. It's a learning process.

What Really Matters

Not knowing how to do something doesn't matter. Focus on your end goal. If you know why you want to achieve your goal, then your reason *why* will drive you forward. You will figure out a way to make it happen. You don't have to have all the details upfront. Your *why* is your inspiration.

Consider the following scenario. Your goal is to lose fifty pounds. How are you going to do it? You are going to eat less and exercise more. How you are going to do it is easy, but the likelihood of you achieving that goal isn't high if you don't have a strong reason why you are doing it. If the reason is that you want to be able to coach your child's team or be able to play with them without getting tired so quickly, now you have a *why*. Merely wanting to lose weight because your doctor told you that you're overweight isn't much motivation.

When you don't have a *why*, you are more likely to fall off the wagon. When your *why* is unclear, it becomes more difficult to maintain growth. With a lack of clarity, the motivation will wear off, and you'll feel like you have to force yourself to stay on track. When you are motivated by your *why*, there is no force needed. You'll spring out of bed inspired to start your day.

If I ask you what your *why* is and you say it's money, I want you to realize that money is pieces of paper. So let's ask the question again. Why do you want money? You might say so you don't have to worry about bills, and you wish to pay off your debt. Let me ask again. Why do you want to not worry and be able to pay off your bills? You might answer that you don't want to feel stressed. So I will ask again, why don't you want to feel stressed? You would answer that you don't want the stress to affect your health and your relationship with your spouse. Can you see where I am going with this? Your why isn't really about money. It's about living a happy and healthy life with your spouse. Money is just one way to get you to what you want.

When you know what your end goal is, then you can figure out the *how*. If you have to know the *how* first, you will be more likely to procrastinate or not start at all. There is no perfect roadmap to success. The road you take may be different than the one I choose. Decide what's important to you. Define the outcome you seek. Commit to achieving it, and then go to work to figure out the *how*.

Ask Yourself

1. In what areas of my life do I use the excuse *I don't know how?*

2. How are my *I don't know how* excuses stopping me from reaching my goals?

3. What goals are important to me? Make a list.

4. Why are these goals important to me?

CHAPTER FOUR
I'll Do It When...

"To do anything in this world worth doing, we must not stand back shivering and thinking of the cold and danger, but jump in and scramble through as well as we can."

— *Sydney Smith*

Moving Forward

WHEN I WAS in the hospital, the thought of *I'll do it when* didn't enter my mind. I wanted to do and learn everything I could now. The only time I had to wait to move forward was because of a physical ailment, or I had to wait for something to be built or the prosthetics to be delivered. I had the will to survive. I was and still am determined to succeed in life. I want to thrive monetarily, as a human being, and as a member of society. That was what pushed me.

People see me at the store or out in public and stop me to talk about what caused the loss of my hands. They notice how easily I use my prosthetics, and they compliment me. People find it an inspiration that I operate so efficiently, and that I didn't let my accident keep me hiding at home from the real world.

There's too much life to live to stay inside. It's a metaphor. Excuses are what keep you stuck inside a lonely house, not living your life to the fullest. Is it easy to venture out? Maybe not. But if you don't, the alternative can be a sad, lonely life of regret.

A friend of mine that was a superintendent for an electric department at a utility company called me and asked if I would come over to speak to his guys that do line work. He wanted me to talk to them about how my accident happened. I agreed and showed up to tell them my story.

Then, a few weeks later, my friend called again and asked me if I wanted to go to a Tennessee Valley Public Power Association meeting. I agreed, and we went. At the end of the meeting, the executive director came over and spoke with my friend and me. By the end of our conversation, he asked me if I would come back for next year's meeting and do the keynote for their conference. I looked around because I thought he was talking to somebody else. When I realized he was asking me, I said "no." I thought to myself, "I'm a lineman, not a speaker." He was insistent and asked me to come back to tell my story. I had a year to prepare for this so in the end, I agreed.

When I came back the next year, I stood up and told my story just like I was asked to do. As soon as I finished, I stepped off the stage, and people started sticking business cards in my pocket. After that, I had my own cards made with my name, email, phone number, and the phrase, "Triumph Over Tragedy." That's how my speaking career started. It wasn't something I was looking to find. If I would have gone with the mindset that *I'll do it when* I become trained, it's not likely I would have pursued this opportunity. I almost let the excuse of not being a trained speaker get in the way of the chance to touch the lives of so many people. I figured it out along the way. I took a few courses and now have a lucrative speaking business. I love what I do.

The Truth about *I'll Do It When*

I'll do it when is an excuse that means *I'll do it never*. This excuse deludes your mind into believing you are going to go for the gold when you are older, when the kids move out, when you have more money, when you get out of your current romantic relationship, when you lose the weight, or whatever story you tell yourself to not take action now. This excuse reinforces procrastination, which ultimately leads to falsely believing you might take action someday when you are more prepared. You hope that your future self will have more confidence or more skills to take on the challenge. The day never arrives, and you are left feeling regretful.

What many people do is hope and wish for their dreams to come true. When that doesn't work, they are disappointed and make excuses about why they didn't get what they wanted. They aren't aware of the thought patterns that keep them stuck.

It takes commitment and discipline to reach your goals. If you find yourself falling into this category, right now, set a deadline and put it on your calendar. Make a detailed plan of action. Then, start even if it is only baby steps. A step forward, no matter what size, is still a step forward. Don't over complicate it.

Most people are not aware of the excuses they make. They don't understand how their thinking is holding them back. To overcome the *I'll do it when* thinking pattern, you first have to become aware of it. Once you become aware of your thoughts of excuses, you can interrupt them. As you increase your awareness, you can make a choice to rid yourself of an excuse mindset.

You have to develop the skill of observing your thoughts, feelings, and emotions in the moment. This is how you change your habits. You have to decide how you want to think and feel. Consider how excuses cause you to feel. Is that what you want your emotional state to be, or is there a more favorable alternative you are seeking? Your decision of how you want to feel and act is the switch that needs to be flipped to change your life.

If you are not in a *no excuses* mindset, it's not likely you will take action. You might think you want to achieve a task, but if you are not committed, you won't take consistent, focused action. To change your habits, it takes time and practice. With the repetition of new habits, the old ones will fade. Consistency means you don't take days off. There is no cheating. You may have to get creative to be persistent. Reward yourself for progress. Most importantly, stay focused on the benefits of achieving your goals.

Excuses are a choice. The more awareness you achieve, the better chance you have to change your mindset and your habits. You can do it when you think your ready or you can do it now. The choice is yours.

Ask Yourself

1. In what areas of my life do I use the excuse *I'll do it when?*

2. How are my *I'll Do It When* excuses stopping me from reaching my goals?

3. What new habit will I commit to implementing? What is my plan for achieving it?

CHAPTER FIVE
Yeah, But...

"The victim mindset dilutes the human potential. By not accepting personal responsibility for our circumstances, we greatly reduce our power to change them."

—Steve Maraboli

It Was My Fault

MY ACCIDENT COULD have been avoided. I could have followed the safety guidelines and wore my personal protective equipment. The gloves I was supposed to wear were rated for high voltages. Twenty-five years ago, the mentality for safety wasn't the same as it is today. It was common to wear leather gloves when working on low voltage wires. The key phrase is *common practice*. Common practice isn't what was written in the safety manual. It's what many of the workers do commonly when working in my situation. What the safety manual said is that if you are within reaching distance of a primary conductor, you will wear your primary voltage gloves.

I made a conscious decision to wear my leather gloves. I walked past the bin that held my rubber gloves and didn't pick them up. My mind was on working on the low voltage conductors. I got complacent and forgot what was behind me. There was no room for a *yeah, but* excuse. I take complete responsibility for my actions.

My mistake didn't only change my life. It affected my family, friends, my coworkers, and my medical team. I accept responsibility for my actions, and I am so grateful to be able to tell my story to help others understand why occupational safety is essential. Today, I speak for companies all over the world teaching safety and personal responsibility. It's not just your life that is affected by an injury like this. My coworkers had to pull me out of the bucket. They didn't know if I would survive. They saw the gloves pulled off my burned hands. It wasn't a pretty sight.

When my parents came to the hospital, they were very distraught. The doctor explained the situation to my parents. My dad tried to convince the doctor to bring him upstairs immediately to amputate his left hand to give to me. I was left-handed, and my dad was right-handed. It seemed like the logical thing to do to help his son. My mistake affected my father so much that he was willing to give me one of his hands.

We all have choices to make in life. Sometimes there are positive consequences and sometimes there are not. When you make a choice, you play a role in the responsibly of the outcome. To live life without excuses, you have to take personal responsibility for everything in your life and not in your life.

The Truth About *Yeah, But*

Yeah, but is an excuse that is one of the biggest sabotages for people. Using the *yeah, but* excuse is a way to refuse any insight or possibility of accomplishing a goal. You are, in essence, rationalizing why you can't succeed. This excuse is a deflection to taking responsibility. Consider the following excuses.

"Yeah, but she never had children. I can't be as fit as her."

"Yeah, I'd like to own my own business, but I don't have the time."

"Yeah, but I love bread too much. I'll never be thin."

"Yeah, but I don't have the money to go back to school."

For the first excuse above, the truth is being fit takes work. It takes daily action. Telling yourself you will never reach your goal before starting is a blatant example of self-sabotage.

What about the second example? We all have the same amount of time each day. What's really going on in this excuse? It's likely the person isn't willing to put in the extra effort to move from being an employee to being a business owner. Saying you don't have the time is an easy out. Consider your priorities. If you really want to own your own business, what are you willing to sacrifice upfront to reach your end goal?

The same goes for the example about eating bread. Do you want to be thin or do you want to eat bread? What is your end goal? Not wanting to give up eating bread isn't a valid excuse to not eat nutritious food.

How many times have you used the excuse, "I don't have the money?" I bet if you got two flat tires and had to replace them to get to work, you'd find the money. If you want something bad enough, you'll find a way. You'll sell something, cut someone's lawn, babysit, take one extra shift, or get a loan. *Yeah, but* is an excuse not to do something, but it's not a good reason.

Working out is one of my daily tasks. It would be easy for me to say, "Yeah, but... I can't lift weights because I don't have hands." Because I am determined to take care of my body, I had to convince my insurance company to give me a pair of workout prosthetics. I have several different pairs that assist me to do different exercises. I couldn't physically bench press until I got them. I can't use free weights, so I use machines. It still accomplishes the same goal to keep my body in great physical shape and physically fit.

Here's the lesson. The next time you attempt to use the *yeah, but* excuse, try saying this instead: "Yeah, I would like to reach that goal, but I am not willing to put in the effort to reach it. Then see how that feels. If you don't like how it feels, try this alternative: "Yeah, it's going to be challenging, but I am committed to putting in the effort it takes to reach my goal." How does that feel? Then you get to choose which course you take.

Stop Complaining

Yeah, but can morph into complaining. It's easy to complain about what's not going right in your life. Many people get sucked into an addictive cycle of blaming and complaining. It's a way to deflect responsibility. When stress builds up, you may need a venting session. But, there is a difference between venting and complaining. There is also a difference between making an observation and unloading on someone.

Complaining can give you the illusion of control, especially if you fear confronting an issue directly. Many times, complainers are looking for sympathy. They need validation for being wronged.

Complaining tends to be chronic for many people. Frustration mounts and then overflows into other areas of your life. Complaining doesn't make the situation better. It only allows you to blow off some steam. Visit any local happy hour, and you will find a group of coworkers complaining about their boss, policy, procedure, and the biggest brownnoser. You'll hear how unfairly people are treated and all the other injustices of the job.

Complaining is not only a drain on you, but it's also draining to the people around you. It can suck the positive energy out of the room. Negativity breeds negativity. If you want to lead a more positive life, you have to remove the negative situations. Complaining won't solve the problem. Do something about it. Learn to compromise. It's ok to talk about your frustration and let people know how you feel. The goal is to create positive change and find a resolution.

Personal Responsibility

Where you are right now in your life is a result of your actions or lack of taking action. Taking personal responsibility for everything in your life and not in your life is the foundation for a life with no excuses. It's the foundation for personal development.

No one is coming to save you. Your white knight isn't gallantly riding to your rescue. Superman isn't going to swoop in at the last minute. The winning lotto numbers aren't going to show up. You have to be your own hero.

Living in resistance to personal responsibility will render you a powerless victim. You'll say things like, "Of course... this always happens to me." When you claim responsibility, you take back your power to affect your results. You no longer blame your problems on external circumstances. It's up to you to make things happen in your life. When you can accept that truth, then you can begin the process of change.

The alternative is making excuses and deflecting that you have the power to make your life what you want it to be. It takes self-discipline to accept responsibility and set yourself on a course of action to release excuses. When you accept responsibility for your life, you accept responsibility for your happiness. Why would you want to give someone else control over your happiness? When you fall into that trap, you are setting yourself up for disappointment.

Happiness is an inside job. You may not make the income you desire yet, or you may not have found the significant other of your dreams, but that doesn't mean you have to be miserable. It comes down to how you filter the situations that happen. When you come from acceptance, then your anger, resentment, guilt, and other negative emotions will fade. From acceptance, you can begin to focus on the solution rather than the problem. You can look for a resolution.

Remember, you are human. Perfection is not part of the happiness equation. Trust yourself to handle whatever comes your way. Be willing to stay the course. Listen to your heart. Get in touch with your inner guidance. The more negativity you remove from your life, the happier you will be.

One thing you have to learn is that to be happy, you can't depend on another person. Your happiness depends on you. It comes from within. We all have shortcomings and weaknesses. We all have painful events that have happened to us. My story is the fact that I lost both of my hands due to an injury where I created the situation for it to happen. I had to forgive myself and accept my circumstances. I haven't let this accident get in the way of becoming successful. I'm still on that journey. Every day is a progression for me to get there.

Ask Yourself

1. What do I complain about most often?

2. In what situations to I tend to feel like a victim?

3. In what areas of my life do I require taking more personal responsibility?

4. How does my mindset have to shift to make these changes?

CHAPTER SIX
I Might Fail...

"I've missed more than 9000 shots in my career. I've lost almost 300 games. 26 times, I've been trusted to take the game winning shot and missed. I've failed over and over and over again in my life. And that is why I succeed."

— *Michael Jordan*

Pressing Forward

YOU MIGHT SAY I failed at my job the day I ignored taking the proper safety precautions. You could also say I failed to protect myself. The truth of the matter is that I don't see it as a personal failure or see myself as a failure. Mistakes happen, and then we have a choice. We can repeat them, we can learn from them, or we can decide to abandon the mission all together and do nothing. We can wallow in the failure, or we can use it to push us harder to overcome the challenge. We can make failure our identity, or we can become our own hero.

Since my accident, I have continued to press forward with faith and hope. I make the best of each day, and I live in gratitude for the opportunity to continue my journey on this Earth. I put my heart and passion into being the best I can be. I don't want the world to see me as a bilateral below elbow amputee. I want the world to see me as an outstanding individual that didn't give up. I want to be a source of inspiration that shows people that even when you have the toughest of situations to overcome, you can do it.

In 2006, Pastor Rick Warren, author of *The Purpose Driven Life*, delivered a TED Talk. He asked the audience to consider what they have been given: talent, background, education, freedom, creativity. He said that it was the primary question about life. He talked about how we are shaped with spiritual gifts, heart, ability, personality, and experiences. He then asked, "Why would God wire you to do something and then not have you do it?" He also said, "Did you know God smiles when you be you?"[2]

Everything that I have done in my life has led me to the point where I am today.

I believe God had a purpose for me on August 12, 1991. Over thirteen thousand volts of electricity passed through my body and I didn't die. I believe my purpose is to be a shining light to other people. I not only impact people by speaking about occupational safety, but when my friends, family, and audiences see how I live a life with no excuses, I genuinely believe it inspires them to do the same. Everything that I have done in my life has led me to the point where I am today. I embrace the successes and the failures.

When you fear failure, you place limits on what you can achieve. Everyone has a mountain to climb in his or her life. There are peaks and valleys. No one is playing on a flat surface. The peaks and valleys are what make life interesting. See the valleys as a challenge and work your way up to the peaks. Every day you forge ahead, you'll become a stronger, more well-rounded human being. It's determination that drives your destiny.

You have four choices when you face a challenge that seems

like a mountain. You can climb it and go straight over the top. You can walk around it. You can blast right through it like dynamite, or you can take the fourth option. You can let the fear overcome you and set up camp at the bottom of the mountain. You can make that place be your new home where you stay for the rest of your life. There's nothing wrong with being afraid. Everyone encounters fear at one time or another. The key is not to let it take over. If you let fear win, you will sacrifice your dreams.

The Truth about *I Might Fail...*

At the heart of the *I might fail* excuse is the motivation to avoid pain. We see failing as painful. To avoid the perceived discomfort, we procrastinate or don't take action at all. The story you tell yourself may be that you aren't capable of achieving your goal, so why try.

The upfront excuses can be a way to justify not succeeding. If you believe you are going to fail, you probably will. It's a self-fulfilling prophecy. What would happen if an athletic team showed up to a championship game with the mindset thinking that they were going to lose? The likelihood of them winning would be low.

To overcome the fear of failure, you first have to own the fear. Journal about it or verbalize it to someone you trust. Don't let the fear simmer in your mind. The longer you ignore your feelings, the more likely you are to procrastinate.

You won't be able to control everything that you face, so focus on what you can control. You can educate yourself and take action steps daily toward your goals. When a challenge arises, focus on a solution. Remember, the only way you fail is by giving up.

Begin to redefine failure. Life is a learning process. Shift your perspective. Let your inspiration to succeed be stronger than your fear of failure. Be willing to take risks. Your fear of avoiding failure can end in the pain of regret. You have one life to live, so go after your dreams.

Limiting Beliefs

What you believe affects how you perceive the world. Your beliefs vastly influence what you think is possible in your life. It's your beliefs that will either propel you to take action or remain stagnant. Most people don't question their beliefs, but this is necessary if you want to live a no excuses life.

Where do you find yourself making the most excuses in your life right now? Examine the beliefs that lead to the excuses you create. Often, the beliefs you hold have been handed down to you by a parent, relative, teacher, friend, religion, or society. Make a list of all the beliefs you have surrounding the most critical area of your life you want to change. Identify the beliefs from the list that are holding you back. Now, imagine how your behavior would change if your beliefs matched your intentions for positive change. You have the power to choose what you believe. If you don't like what you see on your list, go to work changing your beliefs to new and empowering ones.

Changing your beliefs typically doesn't happen overnight. It can take time to change what has been there for so long. Check in with yourself from time to time to see how your beliefs are changing. Read books, listen to audios, go to a seminar, or take a course to assist you with the personal development process. When I started my speaking career, I wasn't trained. To change my belief that I wasn't good enough to be a speaker, I took a few classes. I practiced, and I was willing to give myself time to become good. Life is not about perfection. It's about progress.

Ask Yourself

1. In what areas of my life am I using the excuse *I might fail?*

2. What triggers me to feel *I might fail?*

3. What limiting beliefs or events from my past trigger me to feel *I might fail?*

4. What limiting beliefs will I replace?

5. What new beliefs will I adopt?

CHAPTER SEVEN
I'm Afraid of What People Will Think...

"I cannot give you the formula for success, but I can give you the formula for failure, which is: Try to please everybody."

— *Herbert Swope*

Stepping Outside

URING MY TWENTY-THREE days in the hospital, I never saw how I looked. There were no mirrors in the burn unit. In my mind, I looked the same. The first time I saw myself in a mirror after the accident was at my maternal grandmother's funeral. She passed away while I was recovering in the hospital. I wasn't able to visit her or say goodbye even though she was in a hospital just a few blocks from my burn unit. Not only was I processing what had happened to me, but I also had to process my grandmother's passing. This was a challenging time for my family.

My arms were taped where the amputation had taken place, and I had a port in my chest for easy access for blood draws and injections. I had lost a lot of weight during my hospital stay. My clothes didn't fit anymore. To attend my grandmother's funeral, my father bought me a white short sleeve shirt to wear. This was the first time I had left the hospital since my accident.

When I arrived, I remember walking by myself down the hallway to pay my respects to my grandmother. I came across a mirror hanging on the wall. It took me a moment to realize who I was seeing. It struck me as funny when I looked at it. I was shaggy and rough now. At this moment, I realized how much my appearance had changed. It took me a few minutes to adapt to what I was seeing. I realized people were going to view me differently now. Since this was the first time my family and friends were going to see me, I figured they would feel sorry for me and try to take care of me. They did, but the grief for my grandmother overrode any real concern for how people would react to me.

After I had time to heal, and I went back to work, I not only encountered my coworkers' discomfort of seeing me without hands, but I also had to interact with the public. When I showed up knocking at their door to explain the work that was going to be done for a customer, I could tell by the look in his or her eye they weren't expecting someone like me. Sometimes people would get a real shock when I would shake their hand. They'd feel steel, and if they hadn't noticed my prosthetics, it would scare the heck out of them.

I didn't let any of this stop me from working. I knew it would take time to get acclimated to my new life. I realized it would be uncomfortable in the beginning. Overall, it has helped me to build emotional resilience. I've learned to roll with the punches. One thing my accident has taught me is that you have to adapt to the situations thrown your way. My emotional awareness and willingness to preserve have strengthened on my journey. When all else fails, I'm able to have a sense of humor about life. Your desire to live your best life has to trump your fears. This is how you overcome excuses. Your willingness to live your dreams has to be strong enough to win in the face of fear and doubt.

The Truth About *I'm Afraid Of What People Will Think*

When I go out into public to do the day-to-day errands, people watch me. They take a second glance and sometimes they'll stare. Is it uncomfortable at times? It used to be, but I'm not willing to let the curious nature of people be an excuse not to get out and live my life. If I had let that hold me back, I wouldn't be living the life I am today. I wouldn't have the career I have today. Standing still is not an option I was willing to take.

My occupational therapist told me that people would perceive me based on how I carried myself. If I carried myself as poor pitiful me, then that is how people would treat me. I don't consider myself handicapped. I have a physical challenge with no hands, but it doesn't handicap me. That is how I carry myself.

If I lived my life concerned about what people think, I wouldn't be living my life to the fullest. Since my accident, I've earned my private pilot's license, gone skydiving, and I travel almost weekly speaking all over the United States and sometimes internationally. If there's a challenge, I'll overcome it. What I want people to understand is that I'm a determined man who's living an amazing life.

When you fear what other people think, you assume you know what's in their mind. You make up stories about what they think about you or what they will say when you interact with them. Your concern for how someone will react to your actions, decisions, and words can be the precursor to the creation of an excuse. The fear of what people will think prompts a reason not to take a course of action. This is how you play small in life.

You don't go after your dream job or business because it might make someone feel bad that you make more money than them. You don't progress forward because gaining status would make someone else jealous and feel beneath you.

Don't keep yourself where you are to please someone else. You have one life to live. You are not responsible for other people's feelings. We all have to overcome our thoughts and emotions. Stay focused on yourself and your path.

I recently read an online Inc. article where Sebastian Bailey, Co-Founder and President of the U.S. branch of Mind Gym, was interviewed about how science says your brain can hold you back from success. He gave a demonstration by asking people if they thought a shark or a horse was more deadly. Most people answered the shark was more deadly. When they searched their minds for memories, media stories of shark attacks arose. Because we read and hear about shark stories more often, our brain makes the assumptions that they harm more people than horses. In actuality, there are twenty times more deaths by horses than sharks. Sebastian suggested becoming more aware of your tendencies to be biased to help you make better decisions on your road to success.[3]

Your brain looks for ways to keep you safe. It not only wants to keep you physically safe but also emotionally safe. This is why your bias can play a role in your concern for what other people think. The truth is, it's not beneficial to believe all of your thoughts. You have to question them. Explore your motivations and your excuses.

People Pleasing

When you are afraid of what other people will think, people-pleasing tendencies are often the result. This behavior is rooted in a lack of self-worth. You have a limiting belief that your worth is determined by how well you please others or how well they like you. What tends to happen if you are a people pleaser is that you will do more for others than you will do for yourself. You control people by behaving the way you think they want you to behave so they will like you and praise you.

People pleasers don't like to feel negative feelings. They avoid how uncomfortable it feels to say "no" or to set boundaries and hold people to them. They do whatever they can to keep the peace, even if that means they overextend themselves in some way. People pleasers hold themselves responsible for how other people feel, but this is false.

To release people pleaser tendencies, remember that you are only responsible for yourself. That includes how you feel. This ties in with what I have previously discussed about taking personal responsibility for everything in your life. Each of us has to do that. It's not your job to take responsibility for other people's feelings and obligations. You are not responsible for someone else's success or failure. If you overwhelm yourself doing too much for others, you will create the perfect opportunity for excuses to arise. Here are a few examples:

I don't have the time, because I am too busy helping other people.

What if I upset her by saying no?

I might let him down.

I don't like how it feels when someone is angry or disappointed in me.

I don't want to be in conflict with family.

Begin to put yourself first. Learning to say "no" is the simplest place to start. When you say "no" to someone else, you are saying "yes" to yourself. If you feel guilty about that, take some time to explore why you feel that way. Go to work on releasing limiting beliefs surrounding your guilty feelings. Many times, guilt is a learned behavior from childhood or past events. Stay focused on your goals. What is it you want to achieve, and when do you want to achieve it? Schedule in your priorities first. It's one thing to help someone that is in need, and it's another to give away your valuable time in order to get validation for your worth. Self-worth is an inside job.

Ask Yourself

1. In what areas of my life am I using the excuse *I'm afraid of what people will think?*

2. How does being afraid of what people will think hold me back from reaching my goals?

3. How does people pleasing show up in my life?

4. What can I commit to saying "no" to in order to free up time to pursue my goals?

CHAPTER EIGHT
Living an Excuse Free Life

"You do not blame your shadow for the shape of your body: Just the same: Do not blame others for the shape of your experience."

— *Gillian Duce*

Overcoming Obstacles

AFTER MY ACCIDENT, I knew life wasn't going to be easy, but I was determined to face the obstacles. I recognized that it might be overwhelming at times, and it was. I won't lie. Sometimes life was rough, but in my heart, I knew that if I kept persevering, I could take my life back. I could learn to love life and live it to the fullest no matter whether I had hands or not. I'm not the kind of guy to quit, pack up, and go home. I couldn't do that. It isn't who I am.

Every up and down, every mountain and valley, and every page that I turned on my journey taught me lessons. Every challenge you face is a lesson. When you embrace life's experiences, you will inevitably grow. If you ignore the lessons, the universe will keep presenting you will similar challenges until you learn what you are supposed to learn from them. Do you find yourself thinking,

Why does this always happen to me? If that's you, what is the lesson you aren't learning? How do you set yourself up to be in that type of situation?

Think about it this way. If you get pulled over by the highway patrol and get tickets frequently for speeding, there is a lesson to be learned. You can whine and complain about how it isn't fair. You can blame it on the type of car you have or claim to have bad luck. You can make the excuse that the speed limit should be higher or that the officers are just trying to make quota. These excuses are merely deflections from the lesson you could be learning. Here it is. Slow down and follow the speed limit law. When you learn that lesson, you will stop getting tickets. It's simple cause and effect.

Consider how the speeding example relates to areas of your life. Do you get into relationships with the same type of person hoping for a different result? Do you lend money to people that never pay you back and then you feel disappointed? Do you do more for others than you do for yourself and then feel jaded when they don't return the favor? These are all clues. Learn to ask yourself these types of questions to break through your obstacles.

One of the biggest obstacles and lessons I had to learn was to find forgiveness. I had to forgive myself for what happened. I acknowledge I made a mistake. I didn't purposely try to harm myself. If I would've known my actions would result in my accident, my choices would've been different that day. Forgiveness is one of the greatest gifts you can give yourself. It is a true gift of self-love. Without forgiveness, you will live in struggle. You'll let your mistakes be your excuses as to why you don't succeed.

You can't change the past. What you can do is learn from the past, which includes your mistakes and your achievements. Take the past and use it as an educational tool to make yourself better. When you let go of the past and release worrying about the future, you can live right here, right now without any excuses.

Emotional Skills

We are not born with emotional skills. You have to learn them. To let go of excuses, you have to understand the role emotions play in your decision-making process.

When you make decisions from fear, anger, guilt, or shame, you will likely lead an excuse-filled life. When you feel guilt or shame, you have the excuse you are not deserving or not worthy of receiving. When you are angry, you have an excuse for your inappropriate behavior. As you learn to let go of negative emotions, you won't look for an excuse not to pursue your goals and dreams.

Emotional regulation is crucial. When you let your emotions control your behavior, excuses are more likely to become a way of life. It's important to find tools to slow your emotional process down so you can make decisions from a rational state of mind.

Losing my hands was tragic. Believe me, regulating my emotions through the ordeal was challenging. Life as I knew it was over. If I let my feelings run my decision-making process, I could have easily turned to excuses instead of living a full life. But I didn't. I lived one day at a time. I focused on what I had to do to live my new life, one hour, one minute, and one second at a time. I didn't let myself get too far out in the future. I focused on what I could do that day to make my life better.

Living an excuse-free life takes work. It takes personal development. The more you do the inner work, the better you get to know yourself. You will gain clarity about who you are and who you want to be.

The Blame Game

Life can get tough. That's a fact. Heck, it can feel unbearable at times. It's those tough moments when you have to dig deep. You have to decide to focus on a solution. It's easy to blame your spouse, the government, your boss, or your next-door neighbor for your misfortunes and unhappiness. Sinking into despair, victimhood, and self-pity will never set you free.

Blaming others gives you a false sense of control. You get to manipulate the narrative about why circumstances aren't the way you want them to be. Blame protects your ego. It allows you to feel like you are the good guy, and the other person is the bad one. You gain a sense of superiority, which gives your ego a boost.

Blame is a defense mechanism. It's a way to avoid your flaws. It's easier to deflect blame onto an outside source than to accept personal responsibility. The truth is, the more you own your mistakes, the easier it will be to let go of excuses.

Excuses will not get you results. An excuse is your mind's way of finding the guilty party. It feels better to blame something or someone else rather than to find fault in yourself. You will never reach your goals or your dreams by using blame as a tactic. Blame leads to victimhood. When you are a victim, you have no power. What you have is an excuse for your negative behavior.

Blaming is a way to distract yourself from your goals. It's the reason you don't make progress. Let's face it. Life isn't fair. You will encounter injustices. Sometimes bad things happen to good people, and other times, good people make bad choices.

As humans, we are imperfect. Accept it. You don't have to be perfect to live a good life. Mistakes and missteps are an opportunity to learn and grow. The mistake I made causing the loss of my hands was my fault. I have admitted that many times throughout this book. I accept responsibility. But I also take responsibility for my actions after the accident. I choose not to sit idly and let my life pass me by. I may not be able to do a cartwheel to sail through the air, but I can fly an airplane. That's how I embrace life. I have gratitude for each day I receive on this planet.

Every choice you make has a consequence. You have to live with those choices, and sometimes the effects of those choices are unseen. Do I wish I would have followed safety guidelines and wore my rubber gloves? Absolutely! But I don't dwell on that. There's too much life to live. Excuses are easy. Perseverance in the face of tragedy is my triumph.

Mindset

Mindset is everything when it comes to facing excuses. You can see life's bumps in the road as a problem, or you can see them as a challenge. When you make excuses not to do something, you give your power away. You take yourself out of the game. Power comes from inner knowing that you can handle whatever comes your way.

Energy flows where attention goes. What you hold in your mind expands. What thoughts do you keep in your mind most often? If it's fear and doom, then you will be more likely to make excuses. If you hold optimism and solution-oriented thinking, you will be more likely to feel safe and have peace.

When life gets tough, you can curl up in a ball and feel sorry for yourself, or you can face your challenges head-on. Your attitude determines your ability to move forward. Sometimes we have horrific things happen to us. I get it. Not every day is going to be sunshine and rainbows. Challenging times will push you, but the person you become by working through them is a gift.

Think back to a situation that was challenging for you. To overcome that situation, what did you have to do that was outside of your comfort zone? How did you grow? What did you learn? What is the gift that came out of the situation? You may be thinking that there is no gift in a tragedy. Let's look at my situation.

What gift came out of me losing my hands? I improved my problem-solving skills. I became an example for other people who have lost hope. I teach people all over the United States the importance of how to be safe on the job. I am a shining example of what it means to live a no excuses life. My focus is on what I gained from the experience, not what I lost.

When something happens to us, we have thoughts about the event. Those thoughts can be positive, negative, or neutral. The thoughts result in a feeling or emotional state. How you feel can affect how you react. Have you ever gotten into an argument with someone that made you so angry it stopped you from being productive? Have you ever sent a nasty email or text out of anger? When you get caught up in your emotions, it can limit your ability to make forward progress.

Some events and situations can be devastating and tragic when they happen in your life. Having adverse reactions is normal, but it's how long you stay in that emotional state that makes the difference. When you get caught up in a negative emotional state for an extended period of time, excuses will flow more freely. Your thoughts about the event and how you view life can keep you stuck living in misery and disappointment.

Have you ever met someone who has gone through an adversarial divorce, lost a large sum of money, or didn't make the cut for a team and is still bitter, angry, and resentful years later? That person has let the event rule their life. You have to think better thoughts to change your situation. Let go of the past. You can't change it, but you can absolutely learn from it. Anger and bitterness are excuses to play small.

Marianne Williamson made the term 'playing small' popular with her poem, *Our Deepest Fear*.

You are a child of God. Your playing small does not serve the world. There is nothing enlightened about shrinking so that other people won't feel insecure around you. We are all meant to shine, as children do. We were born to make manifest the glory of God that is within us. It's not just in some of us; it's in everyone. And as we let our own light shine, we unconsciously give other people permission to do the same. As we are liberated from our own fear, our presence automatically liberates others.[4]

I can tell my story by the facts of what happened. It doesn't make me angry, sad, or upset. I am objective. I let go of the emotional attachment to the tragedy, and I replaced it with thoughts of hope and triumph. Reframe your misfortunes to change your perception of the events. When you change your perception, you change your reality.

Be willing to play big in your life, not small. Shift your mindset to think on a grander scale. What would add more joy to your life? Who do you want to be? How do you want to live? Who do you want to serve? When you ask yourself these questions, you open your mind to explore the amazing opportunities life has to offer.

Your Circle of Influence

Are you happy with the people that are surrounding you? If you spend time with people who complain, make excuses, don't have a purpose, or live in victim mentality, you likely will have a similar mindset. As part of taking personal responsibility, you have to realize that you are responsible for your circle of influence. You attracted these people to your life.

As you adopt a new attitude about how you lead your life,

the people you attract will start to change. A person who leads a no excuses lifestyle won't be comfortable around people who live in the drudge of life. It will be challenging to listen to someone complain all the time or stay stuck in their problems.

If you are in the process of transformation, your friends and family may feel uncomfortable with the changes you are making. They are used to you being and acting a certain way. When you start to change, you are becoming a new version of yourself. You will interact with the world differently. What you once would complain about over a cup of coffee with a friend is no longer appealing to you. Your friends and family may feel as if they don't know you anymore. You no longer relate to them the same way. Often, these friends and family members tend to fade away. New people enter your life that are attracted to who you are becoming. Since like attracts like, you attract more positive people.

If there is a person in your life that brings you down with their negative attitude, you have the choice to spend your time elsewhere. You don't have to be a victim of their emotional state. You don't have to listen to them whine, complain, or go on angry tirades. I'm not saying you have to shut everyone out, but you can set boundaries for what you will allow in your life. When you are surrounded by negativity, it is challenging to see opportunities and feel positive. Distance yourself from negativity so you can change your thoughts, habits, and routines to reflect the positive life you envision.

As you begin to live a no excuses life, you set an example for the people around you. Even if your current circle of influence is uncomfortable with the changes you make, over time, they will see how your life has been enhanced. The people that are meant to be in your life will stick around. Just as Marianne Williamson said in her poem, *"as we let our own light shine, we unconsciously give other people permission to do the same. As we are liberated from our own fear, our presence automatically liberates others."* Give yourself permission to be the shining light that touches your circle of influence and sets the example for living with no excuses.

Finding a New Normal

After my accident, I told my physical therapist that I wanted to go back to being normal. She asked me what I considered normal. To me, it meant going back to being who I was before my accident. In reality, going back to what was once my normal is not possible. It wasn't physically possible, and mentally, I couldn't undo what had been done either. Who I used to be was gone, and I had to accept that fact to move forward with my life. What about your life? Is there something you are not accepting that keeps you stuck and making excuses to stay where you are?

We all have challenges. Some are easily visible, and some are not. You can look at me and see how I have been physically changed. You can see my challenges. What many of us don't understand is the mental and emotional challenges. You never know what battles people have been through or are going through. Emotional trauma can be just as devastating as losing your hands. It can change who you are and your ability to function in the world.

Besides not having the function of my hands, what many people don't realize is that I lost my primary sense of touch. Physical contact is a human need. I'm not able to caress my wife's face, and I am not able to feel the tiny grip of my grandchild's hand around my finger. Growing up, I was taught that you learn a lot about someone from their handshake. I still shake hands with the people I meet, but I don't receive the sensory feedback from the exchange. The other person only feels a piece of cold steel from my prosthetic hook. Many years have passed since my amputation surgery, but losing the ability to feel human contact through my hands is more challenging at times than losing the mobility of them. It's a part of life I've had to accept.

My physical therapist told me that the world was not going to change because I got hurt. I had to learn how to adapt to the world the way it was. I had to develop a new normal. I wear short sleeves, and my arms are exposed for everyone to see. I don't hide them. I explain what happened to me if someone asks. I expect people to look, stare, and ask questions. It's not personal. I walk around like everybody else. Like I said before, I shake hands when I meet someone. Not having hands is not my focus, so it becomes less of a focus for the people I encounter. I've even had a friend offer me a pair of gloves when it was cold because they forgot I didn't have hands. My friend could see me for me without being distracted by my prosthetics. I make jokes and find the humor in my situation. I don't give people the opportunity to feel sorry for me. My new normal is to educate, motivate, and inspire people.

You have to create your new normal as well. Your personal challenges or issues are your opportunity to adapt, overcome, and increase your tenacity. When you go through a life changing experience, that's exactly what happens. Your life changes. You can't undo it. You can't unlearn what you have learned, just like you can't unread this book. You have to embrace life no matter what happens because no time machine will take you back to yesterday.

Would I like to have my hands back? Yes, but with the strides I've made, the person I've become, and the character I've built, it would be tough for me to go back to who I was before my accident. I don't know how to be that person anymore. I've learned to see my situation as a blessing instead of a curse. My hope is that my message stays with you as you continue on your journey. It's up to you to live your best life... No Excuses.

Ask Yourself

1. How is my level of emotional regulation? Where can I improve?

2. How does blaming behavior distract me from my goals?

3. What situations or events do I require finding self-forgiveness?

4. How will I change my circle of influence to create positive change in my life?

Notes

1. Fournier, Denise, Ph. D. "Change Your Language, Change Your Life." Psychology Today. February 6, 2019. Accessed May 01, 2019. https://www.psychologytoday. com/us/blog/mindfully-present-fully-alive/201902/ change-your-language-change-your-life.

2. Warren, Rick. TED. Accessed May 27, 2019. https:// www.ted.com/talks/rick_warren_on_a_life_of_purpose/ discussion?language=en.

3. Daum, Kevin. "5 Ways Science Says Your Brain Is Holding You Back From Success." Inc.com. February 03, 2017. Accessed June 22, 2019. https://www.inc.com/kevin-daum/5-ways-science-shows-that-your-brain-is-keeping-you-from-success.html.

4. Williamson, Marianne. Return to Love. (New York, NY: HarperCollins, 1992.), pp. 190-191.

About the Author...

L EE SHELBY IS one of the most sought after motivational and safety speakers today. As a thought leader and best-selling author, he has empowered people around the world through his interactive, educational, and heartfelt conviction. He has the unique ability to combine humor, compassion, and authority to convey his message. As one of  the leading motivational voices of today, Lee relates his occupational injury, his recovery to work, and the challenges he has faced in such a way that will change the hearts and minds of everyone who hears his message.

Book Lee to Speak!

Book Lee as Your Key Note Speaker and
You're Guaranteed to Make Your Event Inspirational,
Motivational, and Actionable!

For over fifteen years, Lee Shelby has been a sought after keynote speaker. His unique ability to deliver an inspiring message with a sense of humor and his Triumph Over Tragedy story empowers audiences around the world.

For More Information – Email Lee@LeeShelby.com

Connect with Lee:

www.leeshelby.com

www.facebook.com/lee.shelby.92

www.linkedin.com/in/leeshelbyenterprises/

Lee's book "Consequences, Workplace Safety is NOT Optional!" debuted on Amazon and became a # 1 Best Seller in 5 different Amazon categories.

"Lee's story is a powerful reminder why workplace safety has to be a daily practice and not just something hidden away in a safety manual somewhere that no one ever opens. He speaks to workplaces all over the world and reminds people why safety matters."

"Very vivid and emotional read of Lee's tragic workplace accident that cost him his two hands. Powerful reminder that your life can change in a second."

Acknowledgments

I EXPRESS MY appreciation to my editor, Carolyn Olson, for the enthusiasm and creativity she brought to this project. Her many helpful suggestions shaped this book.

Thank you to TC Bradley for your support and dedication to promote my story and message.

I also want to thank my occupational therapist, Sandy Fletchall, and my friend, Brian Holland, for being interviewed to contribute to the content of this book.

Finally, I want to express gratitude to my wife Sherrie for her support of this project and her excitement for its release.

UNCENSORED INTERVIEW WITH
LEE SHELBY

Interviewer: How did the accident change you besides having no hands?

Lee: When you have that kind of experience, it can help you to appreciate life more... appreciate the things that you have more. I look forward to every day. It's another challenge. It's another way to do something positive for somebody... to help another person... to be in their life. I never truly thought about being a role model or anything like that. But as time progressed, people tell me that... You know... You really are motivational. You're very inspirational, and that's what I strive to do is create inspiration if I can.

I want to let people know that this is what happened to me. I almost died on this date, August twelfth in nineteen ninety-one. Well, I didn't. And there was a reason why I didn't. You know, God played a big part in that. He wasn't through with me here on this earth. So, you have to hold on to the fact there is a higher power. I had to know that I was left here for a reason, but the accident changed me in a very positive way. Very positive energy came out of that accident, not negative. Granted, there were negative times, but overall, there was very positive energy that came from that accident.

Interviewer: How long were you in the hospital and therapy?

Lee: First let me say, I had no idea whether I would ever make it out. I had no idea what I'd be able to do if I did make it out. Even though I talked to the doctor about cutting my hands off... you have no idea what that means until it actually happens... until you wake up and they are gone... to actually realize that they're not there anymore. So, when you wake up, and you see that... it's very devastating. I did not know how my life was going to end up.

I spent twenty-three days in the intensive care medical burn unit, which was our level one trauma center located in Memphis, in the same city I lived in. When I got out of the hospital, I immediately had to go to therapy that day. They signed my release papers, and Sandy, my occupational therapist, was waiting on me. The therapy unit was attached to the burn unit right next door. The day that I got out of the hospital was the day that I started therapy. Sandy showed me around and what I would be doing. Prior to that, in my twenty-three day stay in the hospital, she would come and see me every day. She would try to stretch my muscles and arms to keep them in good order.

I did the transition into the therapy clinic. I was there for approximately seven months. So, one of the very first things that Sandy would make me do every morning was to work on getting my body built back up. Because, to the best of my recollection when I walked out of the ICU ward, I weighed like 180 pounds. Now, the thing about an ICU ward is the entire time that I was there, especially at the burn unit, I never had any idea what I looked like. I could not see myself because there were no mirrors, and there was a very specific reason for that. They did not want you to see what you look like and be discouraged.

In my mind, I looked the same, except for when I looked down and saw what was not below my elbows. I didn't realize that I hadn't washed my hair. I had a full beard. I hadn't trimmed my beard. I haven't shaved... I hadn't done those things since I'd been in there. I thought I looked like I did when I came in there, but I came to find out that I did not.

Interviewer: What was it like when you first saw your prosthetics for the first time?

Lee: One day, a man walked in the burn unit. He had on a white lab coat. The first thing I noticed was the prosthesis sticking out of the bottom of his jacket. It was a hook just like the ones I have now. All I could see was the hook. I kinda focused on that as he walked up and started talking to me. We talked for a few minutes and the best I can remember, I just kept looking at that hook.

Finally, I asked him, "Is that what I'm going to get? He had pulled up his sleeves and was showing it to me. I asked if that was what was going to replace my hands. He said, "Yes." I said, "Okay." That was the first time I'd ever seen it, and it gave me the sense of making it real. It became real that I was actually going to get something to replace my hands. It was one of those real moments where I realized... Okay... It's not going to be where I am left with nothing. I'm going to have something to function with. I think that was the moment I knew I was going to be okay. I didn't know it at the time, but I was talking to Hector, which was my therapist Sandy's soon to be husband.

Interviewer: What was it like when you first went out in public after your accident?

Lee: People looked at me. People would just stare, and they would want to know what happened to me. Some didn't actually ask me, but they would want to know in their mind what had happened to me. And some would come out and actually ask me, but others would not. People are curious. They want to know why I have a set of mechanical hands, a set of prosthetics, a set of fake arms with hooks instead of your normal hands. The only thing that I did was try to help other people understand.

Interviewer: Who were your biggest supporters through your recovery of your accident?

Lee: That would have been my family. My mom and dad. They were my biggest supporters through this recovery. My daughter wasn't even born yet. But my mother and father were there all the time.

It affected them in ways that I can't even imagine, but they've seen the positive come out of this. They've seen how God has been able to work in my life and do positive things that's come out of this accident.

Interviewer: What was it like going back to work?

Lee: I did not go back and do the same job. You know the thing funny is… I get to thinking about this… the funny part about it is they never offered me that. I knew it wasn't really feasible for me to do line work anymore. Basically, the metal hands and the electricity don't go well together. I went back to work just wanting to work… with the desire to have a job… the desire to do something and desire to be functional and part of the working society again. I didn't want to sit at home. I didn't want someone to take care of me, and I didn't want to be taken care of. I wanted to go back and just be a normal person.

I didn't go back to doing the same job, but I was ready to go back to work. I was busting at the seams to get back to work. I was off work for ten months, and so the timeline was twenty-three days in the hospital, seven months of occupational therapy… but ten months and twenty-three days off of work. So, there is close to four months that I was off work at home by myself doing nothing. I was ready to get out of the house. I was ready to do something.

I could not stand sitting in that house anymore without being around people. Yes, I was ready to go back to work.

When I got back to work, my supervisor gave me a pickup truck and a radio. He told me to go do little things for crews and run errands for crews. And from that point, they started trying to figure out where to put me. They had an idea where they wanted me to end up, which was as an inspector. It took a little time to get into it, and I finally became an inspector.

But going back to work was just a part of the relearning process... of learning how to do everything again and learning how to drive again. I would have to drive all over the city. I'd use my map book to find streets. There was no electronic GPS back then. I had to learn how to use a radio with prosthetics. My radio was a handheld radio. I would have to do certain physical tasks that required me to pick up things and load stuff into the truck or deliver things to crews.

I had to deal with the public too. They had never seen a guy like me come to their door and knock. I had to tell them what was going on with a contract. I had to learn to be a very positive person. I just couldn't walk around with my head down, or you know... be mumbling or talking real low and acting like I didn't want to be there. I just acted like I would have before I ever got hurt. Then people started not to notice my prosthetics as much until they actually looked down and saw that there was nothing there. Or I'd shake hands with them, and I'd scare the hell out of them because they'd have something in their hand they weren't expecting.

Interviewer: Tell me about how you learned to fly an airplane?

Lee: I'm not sure long how many years I'd been back to work, but part of my job duties as an inspector was to inspect all of the steel structures, meaning the towers and the steel poles... everything that carried all of our transmission system in Shelby County. To inspect those steel structures meant that I would go down to the police department where they had helicopters. I would go down there and rent a helicopter. A policeman pilot would fly me three days a week, every other month, and we do it out of a helicopter. I had maps and routes all laid out, and they would fly me, and I would inspect out of the helicopter. I did this for a long time.

I don't really remember how it came about, but I was approached by someone higher than me... some boss somewhere, about some kind of pilot program, or they wanted to investigate alternatives to renting a helicopter because it was very pricey to rent a helicopter and a pilot. They decided to try to do it from an airplane to see if it worked. I was the inspector at the time, so they approached me about taking flying lessons so I could fly over the transmission lines. And I said, "Yeah, I'd love to."

I had to go down to the Olive Branch airport in Olive Branch, Mississippi. They had a nice airport down there with a facility. And my flight instructor that they put me in contact with used to be a gas foreman. He worked at the same company I did it in Memphis, but he was in the gas department. I think he was a gas foreman or job foreman or something like that. I'm not sure of his official title in the gas department, but he was a very good pilot. He had a very extensive logbook.

They hooked me and him up, and we started flying. He and I would just take off and build hours and go places. I eventually learned to fly with no hands, but I didn't have any apparatus or anything that I would use like an assistive device or anything like that. There were challenges to it. The biggest challenge was operating the radio because the radio was... If you know how yoke on an airplane is, it's kind of a big U or a W with it pointing up where you're holding it with both hands. The radio button is a little bitty button on the top where the left hand is. So, when you're holding the yoke in your left hand, your thumb would be able to press that button easily. Well, I couldn't do it, so I had to hold on with one hand and take one hand and press the button to talk. So that was the biggest challenge was learning that.

The airplanes that we flew were relatively brand-new airplanes. A lot of them came equipped with GPS navigational systems in them, but my instructor didn't want me to use the navigation systems. In other words, I used a compass and a map to fly headings because he told me, "One of these days this stuff is going to go out." So, that's what I did. I used the navigation system very little…. hardly ever. But we would just use maps and a compass, and I would make my headings, and I would have to do all my pre-flight checks. I did them just like anyone else would. I did all my pre-flight stuff. I would plan my route. I did all my weight and balance checks of the airplane.

Sometimes, we would fly from the Olive Branch Airport to the Gulf where we could see the shrimp boats, and we would fly down there. Then we'd rent a car and take four or five big coolers, go down the dock and fill them all up with shrimp to bring back with us. We'd have to fly back, which meant that the weight in the airplane was totally different than it was going down there. I had to do a weight and balance check on the airplane again.

I passed my ground school, but one of the biggest things was to get my actual license because I don't have fingerprints. There was just no way to do it. I went up for my check ride to make sure that I could do everything. I got my signed certificate. I got my license, but it took a little bit longer because they had to make sure that a guy with no hands could fly an airplane.

Interviewer: What types of things can't you do because of your prosthetics?

Lee: That's hard for me to say because I figure out another way to do most things if I can't do it like everyone else. When you take any task that you have... like using my phone. I can't use an Apple phone because an Apple is capacitive technology. But I can use an Android. So, with that, I use an Android phone instead of an apple. Would I like to have an iPhone? I don't really care, because I can use my phone to do everything that most Apple iPhones can do, in my opinion.

I had to find another way as far as holding it. I use a lot of wireless Bluetooth. I use earbuds to talk with. I may use my speakerphone phone more than others do because it makes it simpler. Not that I can't take this phone and put it up to my ear, but it makes it simpler for me to maneuver and do everything I have to do without holding the phone. The reality is you can only do two things at a time. I don't have ten fingers, so I can't push buttons and grab things and hold things with two hands.

For my computer, I have a stylus. I have styluses everywhere. Anywhere I go I'm buying two, three, four, five of them at a time. Wherever I'm at a little shop, at the airports, I buy them. I carry a collection of them in my backpack. But I use a stylus to operate my touchpad on my computer. I type... not as fast as somebody that can type with ten fingers, but I do type. I don't make excuses for these things by saying I can't do them. When people tell me to type something and then send it to them... I'm gonna type it and send it to them. I'll fill out all my contracts, all my invoices, and my proposals for my work. I do it. I type it myself. No one else does it for me.

Whenever you think about the things that you do that are really elementary that you use your hands for all the time... I had to learn to do it with prosthetics. Everything that I do takes longer. It's more of an arduous task to get something accomplished. Everything down to tying your shoes. Whatever it is, I can do it, but it takes me longer. That doesn't mean that I'm going to make an excuse for not being able to do it. No. I'm going to do it. I do it happily. I do it really without worrying about how long it's going to take.

This whole process has taught me patience. I did not allow this to teach me the negative aspects of life. I allowed it to play a very positive role in my life, so I could play a positive role in other people's lives.

Interviewer: Were there any psychological aspects of losing your hands that affect you?

Lee: Over the years, especially with the loss of both hands, there is a challenge of not becoming psychologically disengaged from society because I can't touch another human being. With metal hands, I can't put my hand on someone. I can put my hook on them, but I can't put my hand on them.

Hands have receptors that feel. Even though you have nerve endings in every part of your body... your legs, your arms, your face, your feet, but the receptors in your hands can't be replicated. It can't be duplicated in any other part of your body. When you can't feel with your hands, if you allow yourself to, you can get disconnected from society in that way.

One of the things I learned growing up was the importance of shaking hands with people. That's what I was taught to do. When you meet someone, you greet them, look them in the eye, and say hello. You introduce yourself, and you shake hands. You can tell a lot about a person by the way they shake hands... their grip, the way they hold your hand.

For me, I have to find another way to do it because whenever I shake hands with people, all they feel is a piece of steel, and I'll feel someone pulling on the end of prosthetics.

Interviewer: How did you adapt when your first child was born?

Lee: My ex-wife and I were together in Memphis driving, and she had a car wreck which sent her into labor. She said to me, "Whatever you do... do not let that doctor through that door. I don't care what's going on with me. LeAnna is not gonna be born on Halloween." I said, "Alright, whatever." You know I was like... if anything happened, I was going to bar the door, which that wasn't what we were really going to do... So, my daughter was born on November first, right after Halloween.

When LeAnna was born, I had to go back to therapy. I told my therapist, "I'm going to be a father. I don't know how to take care of kids." Because, to be truthful and be honest with you, I had never changed a diaper a day before my life. Never. I'm talking about never. I have no brothers and sisters. I didn't have any other kids to change diapers on. I tell people this story all the time about changing diapers. My buddies, when we were growing up, would get their girlfriend pregnant... I stayed away. I didn't want to catch it. Ha, Ha. I thought... I knew how it happened, but I didn't change their diapers either.

My therapist had me go through this whole diaper changing therapy session on how to take care of kids, and this, that, and the other. I think we started out with a plastic doll and some diapers. I actually have a picture of me with a kid that she brought in for me to kind of handle and practice with. This kid was walking, so he was probably around two years old or something like that. So that's how I learned to diaper my daughter.

I adapted to pick her up and hold her in my arms. I could slip my prostheses off whenever I needed to. In other words, I could just kind of scrunch my shoulder up and slide it off and loosen my harness a little bit. I could slip one arm out and then slip the other one out and then let them dangle off, but my arms would be back to the regular flesh. I could pick her up and maneuver with her. I could move around and do whatever I needed to do, and if I had to slide an arm on, I could just slip my arm back in my prostheses and pick up something to do whatever I needed to do.

Interviewer: Do you have any challenges when you fly to your speaking events?

Lee: My airport routine is kind of like a lot of other routines. Most of the time, when you frequent the same place over and over again, people naturally get to know you well. They get to know me a little bit better than they get to know the average person because I stand out of the crowd a little bit more with no hands. They don't get to see other people with prosthetic hands. Naturally, when I walk into a room, people remember me.

Normally the same people are always working. I always fly on Delta. When I go, I usually see the same guys there at the ticket counter when I go to check in and check my bags. I never have carry-on luggage. I always check my luggage, because I carry an extra set of prostheses in my luggage and carry all my cables… I have a lot of extra stuff that I need to check. So, when I check my luggage, I see the same group of people at the ticket counter when I get my boarding pass.

And then whenever I go to the TSA, I use TSA Precheck… That way, I keep my shoes on. All of this was developed over a period of time. It's not that I wanted to make an excuse for not taking off my shoes. It was because I had to simplify things in my life. In other words, if I wanted to be productive, be efficient, and be professional, I wanted to do what other people did.

TSA Precheck is a simplification for me. It makes things much easier for me to go through TSA than it does if I were to go to the normal line where I would have to unpack my computer and take my shoes off or take my belt off and all that other stuff. I never thought they would let me get it because I didn't have

79

fingerprints, but they did. When I go through my TSA line, I go through the Precheck line and usually a lot of the times the same people are there because I take early morning flights.

When I check in, I don't go through the metal detector… which is like the normal regular metal detector. I go through the body scanner because I always set the metal detector off. So, when I go through the body scanner, they step out, and they have to pat me down. It automatically lights up where all the metal is, which is the harness across my back and my hands. They have to pat me down, and it's just a simple pat down. If there is any other metal that shows up on me… like I've had my belt show up a lot because I keep it on. They also do a chemical swab on my prosthetics. After that, I'm done. So, I can get through TSA really quick… probably almost as fast as the people that are going through the line with me.

I use Clear a lot because I'm registered with that, and that's just the visual. They give you the two options for Clear. You can either use your fingerprints or your retinal scan. I don't have fingerprints, so I use the retinal scan. It's another more efficient way for me to operate. So, any place that I can use that, I use the retinal scan.

Interviewer: Have you always lived a no excuse life, or did the accident change you?

Lee: I was human. I was just like everyone else. I could make excuses for reasons why I didn't do things. It wasn't like it was a really bad habit with me. I wasn't very excuse oriented. But, I'll say I was less likely than other people to make excuses to figure stuff out.

The accident itself very much changed me with making excuses. I learned that I could not make excuses anymore. Over the years, with all the things that I've been through, I realized excuses were just ways of getting out of doing something. They were ways to keep from growing. They were ways to stifle my personal growth.

The accident did change me in that respect. But when you wake up and you realize that you don't have any hands… you start going through therapy, and you start going through rebuilding your entire life around a set of prosthetics and around what you have to deal with just to survive just in the basic simple stuff that life is about… then you realize you can't make excuses for the things that need to be done.

When I got my prosthetics, I had to go back to doing things that I had always done, like going into a store or going to the bank, going to the post office, going to the grocery store or going to do all the things that I'd always done.

I didn't use my prosthetics as an excuse not to get out because I didn't look the same. Whenever I go places, people will watch me. They will look at me. They'll take that second glance, and sometimes they'll stare. Kids basically will, but they're just curious. I didn't use the curious nature of people as an excuse not to get out and live my life.

Interviewer: What kind of hobbies did you have before the accident and were you able to continue them afterward?

Lee: Growing up, I was active. I played athletics in school. I maintained a good physical life. I worked out in the gym. Growing up in the south, I was predisposed to hunting and fishing. That's what we do as our hobbies. I had to relearn all of my hobbies which were hunting, fishing, riding four-wheelers and driving tractors, and things like that… all the things you learn to do down here.

Since the state of Tennessee already had my fingerprints in the system due to some prior youthful activities which involve me and the police... I was able to get my permit. The state of Tennessee actually gave me a handgun carry permit... and the irony is I don't have hands.

The first time I went hunting again after my accident, my father had called me to ask if I wanted to go deer hunting with him. I said yes, and the next morning, we got on our four-wheelers and headed out into the woods. My dad has his own farm, and he has a few hundred acres of woods that he uses for deer hunting.

If you deer hunt, you may use a ladder stand, a climbing stand, or a lock-on stand. My father has a different viewpoint about his comfort level in the woods. He likes to build condominiums in the tops of trees. I'm talking about a ten by ten or twelve by twelve sized room containing the four walls, windows, and roof. Some of them have carpet, a desk chair, and a table. So, I climbed up in one of the condominiums in the woods and my dad climbed up in a different one about a quarter to a half mile away.

So, where we hunt is very thick. Because it's thick, we have to cut out shooting lanes in the woods for us to be to be able to shoot through. There is probably a fifteen to a twenty-foot-wide path where we cut down all the trees and everything in there. This way we can see completely through it. There's no obstructions... no trees, no bushes, nothing in our way. We do that in four or five different directions from where the stand is so we can see all different directions.

Now, I was shooting an old Remington Wood Master 30-06 deer rifle. The magazine holds five shots. You put one in the chamber, so you got six shots. That's what I did. I loaded the magazine myself... loaded all the shells in it, and put one in the chamber, and put the magazine in it.

I was sitting there and watching. I heard a deer come up on my right-hand side, and it was walking... And he was gonna walk directly in front of the middle of a shooting lane. I clicked off the safety and opened the window.

There was a cedar tree behind the deer. When it walked out in front of that cedar tree about 40 yards away... I whistled. When you whistle, the deer stops. So, when it stops, you better be ready to take your shot. That's what I did. I took the shot.

I did not realize what was gonna happen when I pulled that trigger. I didn't pull my hook out of the trigger guard fast enough... It recoiled off my shoulder, and every time it would recoil off my shoulder, it would pull the trigger again and again and again. So, it was an automatic rifle. The shells were flying off the wall of the deer stand that I was in, and it sounded like an automatic rifle. It was just one bam, bam, bam, bam, bam right after another till the gun was empty.

I never did get the deer. I just blew the hell out of a cedar tree that was behind him. There were just cedar pieces going everywhere. I don't know whether it ran away and died of fear or whatever, but I missed the deer.

About two minutes later my father came driving over the hill to my deer stand to see what I had got. He hollered up at me and said, "What did you get?" and I told him to turn around. I asked him, "Do you see that cedar tree about 50 yards away?" He said, "Yeah." I said, "I just blew the crap out of that cedar tree."

One of the other hobbies I had before my accident was fishing. I had to relearn how to do that. I had to learn how to cast a rod and reel, and I had to figure out the right one to use because there are different types of reels that you use when you fish. I can't just use any reel. I have to use a specific reel, which is a spin caster. I found that I can efficiently operate this type of reel.

To relearn, I took a bolt and tied it to the end of the line. I put a bucket at the end of my driveway, and I practiced casting the pole to hit that bucket. That's how I learned when I was a kid, so that's what I went back to for relearning.

Interviewer: You recently were a speaker for a group of high school students. How was that experience?

Lee: Kids are great. Kids are just enormously curious. They love to ask questions, and I love talking to kids. Anytime I get the opportunity to talk to kids, I do. I had one opportunity in Canada recently when I was speaking for Louisiana Pacific. The man that I was there speaking for asked me if I would speak to their vocational high school in town. It was for ninth through twelfth graders.

These kids do welding, electrical, shop classes, carpentry, and just different classes like that. There was stuff there for girls like preparing for beauty school classes... where you learn to fix hair and do things like that. So, there were vocational classes for boys and girls that didn't want to go to college. They just wanted to work. I was asked if I would come to speak to them, so I did.

I met the principal, and she asked me about where my computer was and do I have my PowerPoint. I said, "No, ma'am, I don't have a PowerPoint." She said, "You don't have PowerPoint?" I said, "No ma'am." She said, "How are you going to do this without something visual?" I told her, "I don't need a PowerPoint. I'm all the visual they need." She looked at me for about five seconds. It was an awkward silence. Then she said, "Okay, I guess you know what you doing. These are kids. They're very visual. They need something to keep their attention." I said, "Ma'am, you do not have to worry about a thing. I will keep their attention for the entire time."

There were close to two hundred students in the gymnasium. They were just the most polite group of young people that you can imagine. They asked questions. They were engaged. They wanted to know things. They asked questions about work. I didn't need a PowerPoint for it. I didn't need to give them the PowerPoint that I used for my safety presentations because these kids have never worked before. They didn't need to know what I was telling men and women that have jobs and have worked for X number of years. What they needed to know was how to handle job skills. They needed to be able to talk to employers. They needed to know how to handle things when you don't get a promotion or a job.

How do you handle that loss?

Well, the same way you handle the loss of your hands. You learn to cope with it in a manner that doesn't harm your character. It doesn't define your character or cause you to embarrass yourself... or not to dishonor anything that you've done. Just because that door shut or was taken by another person, that doesn't mean that another job won't open up.

We always try to do things on our own schedule. Things don't always work on our schedule. God has a bigger plan for us than what we understand.

So, talking to kids I find very cool. For me, I love motivating and inspiring them. I let them know that life does not end when a traumatic illness, injury, or something tragic happens.

You get back up. Pick yourself up off the ground, and you go back and carry on. You may not have every faculty that you once had, but carry on with what you have. Make the best life you can make. Be the best version of yourself.

Interviewer: What are your future goals?

Lee: I have the opportunity in April and May of 2020 to go to base camp at Mount Everest. I've talked to the group that is supposed to be going. They said that they approved me to go. I've had several Skype interviews with them. It's supposed to be video documented. So, I am hopefully going to Mount Everest base camp… which is a real feat for someone with no hands.

Right now, I am working toward that goal. I'm working on my getting my cardio up… my strength and conditioning ready to handle everything that involves doing this type of trek. I'm supposed to go do some treks in other mountainous regions here in the U.S. where I can get more in tune before I go to Everest. I am really hoping to make this trip happen.